CURATE

& Flourish

HOW THE WORD OF GOD TRANSFORMS US

by Marjie Schaefer

Thank you!

We are so very grateful for the generous donations given by friends of Flourish. This Bible study is graciously made available through private donations from:

Dr. Gregg Jantz of the Center for Hope

Marc and Marce Nance

www.FlourishThroughTheWord.com

ISBN: 978-1-7328977-5-5

Dedication

I always pray about who the Lord would have me dedicate a new study to and how I could honor them. As I've prayed this time, He seemed to impress upon me to honor those women in my life whose pursuit of Him encourage me to *flourish*.

There's no way I could list all of those women in the pages of this study book.

I choose to highlight the wonderful women of our *Flourish* community both near and far.

Each week, hundreds of women gather to worship, study the Bible, pray and cultivate community. Many gather locally at our host site in Bothell, Washington, while others meet virtually in their homes or other churches. This past season, a group of moms with little ones established their own *flourishing* community using the *Marco Polo* app and they spurred one another on as they took care of their young children.

I love the people of God and I am so grateful to be numbered among them.

May we all continue to curate and flourish as we pursue Jesus in all His fullness!

Hello friend,

Our trajectory as believers is forward and not backward. In other words, the Lord intends for us to *flourish.*

The goal of this study is to dig deep into God's Word and to **curate** or organize, select, and present the truth we have personally studied. From our curating, we are better equipped to **flourish** in our spiritual journey with Jesus.

Someone has said that we become what we behold.

There is simply no escaping the fact that we're conformed to what we focus on. What are you focusing on? Is it your personal desire to flourish spiritually?

If that is your goal, if you want to know joy and peace and to be a fruitful disciple of Jesus, it is important that you are a woman of the Word.

The word **flourish** conveys what life in Christ is meant to be—enjoying the Lord and living for Him; it's serving with gladness and knowing Christ as our greatest delight.

Is this the testimony of your life? Would you say that you have a flourishing lifestyle?

Come join us for this 6-week journey of deeper discovery of Jesus as we unpack the story of the woman at the well, and from there move on to Biblical identity and personal growth as we tackle the issues of life that try to weigh us down.

My prayer for you as you begin this study and give attention to it every day, is that you would meet Jesus in a new and fresh way. May you tap into that living water and **zoe** life that He promises to give to each one of us that belongs to Him.

May your roots go down deep in Him, and may you be forever changed.

For His glory,

Marjie

Lesson One

The Woman at the Well Meets Jesus

Curate:
To select,
organize,
and present
information
gleaned from
expert knowledge.

You will be spending the next three weeks digging through the incredible encounter of Jesus with the woman at the well. This story lays the foundation and groundwork for this Bible study as we see how a woman of shame and dishonor becomes an evangelist for her whole city.

Take the time to read all the Scriptures provided so that you glean the entire context of this unique conversation that not only changed a woman's life, but the lives of countless others.

Prayer Starter: *"Dear Lord, even though this story is familiar to me, I ask You to speak to me in a fresh way as I devote myself to studying it at length. Show me things I've never seen before and cause me to grow in the process. Do in me what only You can do and help me to be a stronger student of Your Word."*

---

1. Read the story of the woman at the well in John 4: 4-42. What specific aspects of this encounter jump out at you as you read? List them here.

2. Jesus asks the woman for a drink in verse 7. What is her immediate response, and why do you think she answered that way? To read the full background story, please visit 2 Kings 17:24-41. The Samaritan woman was well aware of the racial tension between her people and the Jewish people. What particular things do you learn in verses 29 and 33 out of the 2 Kings passage?

Lesson 1, Day 2

Yesterday you spent time getting the context of our story with some additional background information. Today, we will look a little closer at the woman herself. Reread the story in John 4 to answer the questions.

Prayer Starter: *"Dear Lord, thank You for showing me that You can use anyone to accomplish Your kingdom purposes. Thank You for the example of Jesus and His unconditional love."*

1. Why do you think the information in verse 4 is important?

2. Why do you think Jesus chose this Samaritan woman to have this conversation with?

3. What pertinent information do you learn in verse 9?

4. Why do you think the woman wanted to stop coming to the well, as stated in verse 15?

5. What do you think is the purpose of Jesus addressing her husband in verse 16?

6. Verse 18 reveals aspects of the woman's reputation. What else do you learn from this verse, and how do you think the people of that day viewed her?

7. Verse 27 reveals another cultural aspect of the day. What was that?

8. What present-day lessons do you glean from Jesus' bridging the culture gap with this woman, and what does this reveal to you about your Savior and who He reaches out to?

Lesson 1, Day 3

Today you will spend the bulk of your study time 'dissecting' Jesus' answer to the woman's question in verse 10. Read the conversation in John 4:9-10.

Prayer Starter: *"Thank You, Lord, for showing me through the Word how a simple conversation can turn a heart towards You. Continue to speak to me through Your Word today, and may I be used greatly of You to lead others to Your gift of grace in Jesus."*

1. What two components of giving does Jesus reveal in His answer?

2. What is your working definition of grace? Write it out here.

3. Another possible definition of **grace**: God, meeting us at our point of need through the Person of Jesus Christ. Jesus' response to the woman's question is power packed with truth and the revelation of Himself. To glean even more of an understanding of what He was communicating, read Romans 5:15-19.

4. In Romans 5:15, 16, and 18, the phrase "free gift" is mentioned as an aspect of Jesus' salvation of His people. How does this passage align with Jesus' own words in John 4:10 as He talks with the woman?

5. In Romans 5:17, three truths are listed that can change our lives as we embrace this verse by faith.

- How much grace do we receive?

- What additional gift do we receive?

- What does Jesus empower us to do in life?

Lesson 1, Day 4

In the previous day's study, we examined part one of Jesus' two-pronged answer to the woman at the well. Jesus revealed to her the gift of God. Today we will look at the second part of His answer, the 'living water'.

Read John 4:10-18 in preparation for today's questions.

Prayer Starter: *"I thank You, Father, for the gift You have given in Your Son, Jesus Christ. Thank You for this teaching on the living water. Help me to learn more of what it means for me, and enable me through this study to pass it along to others who are longing to go deeper into relationship with You."*

---

1. Look up these verses about 'living water' and briefly summarize each one.

   - Isaiah 12:3:

   - Isaiah 44:3:

   - Isaiah 55:1:

   - Zechariah 13:1:

   - Zechariah 14:8:

   - Jeremiah 2:13:

- Jeremiah 17:13

- Psalm 36:7-9:

2. What new thing have you personally learned about 'living water' from this brief look at some Old Testament verses? Write that out here and put it into a prayer form.

Lesson 1, Day 5

Today we will continue to study the 'living water' and how the woman at the well responded to Jesus as He spoke of it to her.

Read John 4:10-15 and answer the questions for today.

Prayer Starter: *"Father, I thank You so much for providing the living water for me and caring enough that You bid me come and drink. May I learn all the things You have planned for me to learn out of my study of the Word today."*

1. What two things does Jesus promise those who drink from the 'water' He offers?

2. Do you think the woman initially understood Jesus' teaching on the living water? Base your answer on her specific responses.

3. How do verses 10-15 relate to the message of what Jesus is communicating to the woman?

4. Look up the two references listed and summarize each one. Tie these Scriptures in to the story of the woman at the well and her encounter with Jesus.

   • John 7:37-39:

   • Revelation 21:5-7:

Personal Journaling Page
Use this page for your own intentional gratitude,
prayer requests for your group and additional notes.

Personal Journaling Page
Use this page for your own intentional gratitude,
prayer requests for your group and additional notes.

Lesson Two

Zoe Life

Fill My Cup, Lord

Like the woman at the well I was seeking
For things that could not satisfy;
And then I heard my Savior speaking:
"Draw from my well that never shall run dry".

Fill my cup Lord, I lift it up, Lord!
Come and quench this thirsting of my soul;
Bread of heaven, Feed me till I want no more -
Fill my cup, fill it up and make me whole!

There are millions in this world who are craving
The pleasures earthly things afford;
But none can match the wondrous treasure
That I find in Jesus Christ my Lord.

Fill my cup Lord, I lift it up, Lord!
Come and quench this thirsting of my soul;
Bread of heaven, Feed me till I want no more -
Fill my cup, fill it up and make me whole!

So, my brother, if the things this world gave you
Leave hungers that won't pass away,
My blessed Lord will come and save you,
If you kneel to Him and humbly pray:

Fill my cup Lord, I lift it up, Lord!
Come and quench this thirsting of my soul;
Bread of heaven, Feed me till I want no more -
Fill my cup, fill it up and make me whole!

https://www.lyricsmode.com/lyrics/r/religious_music/fill_my_cup_lord.html

This week we will look at many Scriptures that will broaden our understanding of the 'living water' that Jesus spoke of in John 4.

As Christ-followers, most of us would never deny that we do indeed have the Spirit of the Living God, the resurrection power, resident within us. But have we truly grasped this transforming truth at our deepest level to where our lives are characterized by confidence, joy, peace, patience, and power?

Is this our daily experience with the Holy Spirit, or have we mentally assented to His Presence and intellectualized Him?

Have we remained as a stagnant pool when Jesus has promised us 'living water'?

Are we basing what we believe about the Holy Spirit on the comfort of our religious culture and experience, or are we truly living Biblically?

Are you satisfied with the status quo, or does the tantalizing taste of the living water entice you to go deeper with Jesus and all that He offers?

Jesus didn't save us just so we could attend a comfortable church on Sunday, live a moral life, raise well-behaved kids, have a job that is satisfying and sufficient for all our wants and needs, and then glide into our sunset years relatively pain-free.

Jesus saved us for the purpose of intimate relationship with Him by grace, through faith, so that out of this love relationship will flow a partnership with Him to bring the 'living water' to others and to reveal Jesus on the earth today.

The Holy Spirit, or Living Water, operating in our lives at maximum capacity through our blood-bought relationship with Jesus, is what makes us different than any other religion on the earth. Jesus saved us. He fills and equips us.

Prayer Starter: *"Lord, I ask You to make me open and teachable to what the Bible has to say to me today. Enable me to set aside any of my own pre-conceived notions, traditions, or baggage that I may be carrying regarding Your precious Holy Spirit. Teach me more of You."*

---

1. Read John 1:4 and write out the verse below:

2. There are four Greek words in the New Testament translated 'life'. The Greek word that Jesus brought to the world is **zoe.** This means eternal life and the life of God Himself. What did Jesus say about the words He speaks in John 6:63?

3. Read John 10:10 and write out from Jesus' words the *what and the type* of **zoe** Jesus came to bring.

Paul had plenty to say about the *zoe* life as well. *Zoe* enables us to be more than conquerors and transforms us from glory to glory. *Zoe* is the source of grace and gives us wisdom. Look up the following Scriptures and answer the questions below.

Prayer Starter: *"Lord, teach me more about life in Your Spirit. Speak to me specifically out of Your Word."*

1. In Ephesians 3:19, what did Paul pray for Christians?

2. By filling us with His own life, God Himself becomes our life, peace, righteousness, purity, strength and health. The Holy Spirit is our zeal, our guide, our teacher - everything we need for life and godliness. How is this possible? Write out your answer based on Romans 5:10.

3. All the abundant *zoe* life is made possible through the precious blood of Jesus, shed for us on the cross. Take a few moments to thank Him and worship Him for who He is and what He has done for you. Write out your praise below.

4. Write out an abbreviated version of how you came to Christ and what He means to you today. Pray for an opportunity to share your story this week.

The Vine's life (*zoe*) is in the branches; the life of the branches is directly connected to the Vine. Jesus desires that all His branches be full of His own life (*zoe*).

"He who is joined to the Lord is one spirit with Him." (I Corinthians 6:17)

Read John 15:1-11 for today.

___

Prayer Starter: *"Lord, thank You for making Your zoe life available to me. Thank You for giving such clear direction in Your Word so that I can thrive in my relationship with You."*

___

1. Jesus calls Himself_____ (verse 1) and His Father is the _____ (verse 1). Jesus calls us _____(verse 5).

2. According to verse 4, what is the key to bearing fruit?

3. In verse 5, what are we able to do without the true vine?

4. When we abide in Christ (from John 15):

   Our prayers are _____. Verse 7

   We glorify _____. Verse 8

   We keep His _____. Verse 10

   We abide in His _____. Verse 10

   We have full _____. Verse 11

Lesson 2, Day 4

A healthy vine produces great 'fruits' that result from healthy *zoe* life. Read Galatians 5: 22-26 for today.

Prayer Starter: *"Lord, I thank You that You enable me to produce healthy fruit in my spiritual life and walk with You. Thank You for providing a handbook that teaches me daily how to live. Thank You for Your Word and for how practical it is."*

1. Write out the 9 fruits of the Spirit and tell how each one is a result of a healthy harvest with the Lord.

2. Jesus used practical illustrations and word pictures to teach the agrarian people of His day the truths of who He is. The Vine and the branches bearing spiritual fruit is a classic example of this. Since all His examples are preserved for us in Scripture, the illustration is meant to teach us through the ages. Paul continued Jesus' practice by providing another word picture. Use this space to draw a picture of a healthy vine or healthy tree producing the *zoe* life of the fruits of the Spirit.

Jesus has promised us the fullness of Himself as we remain in Him. This is our inheritance in Christ. Whenever we sense a lack, we pray to the Giver of *Zoe*, the Vine life, the Living Water, Who produces fruit in us, and He gives more of Himself.

Read Galatians 2:20-21 and Galatians 3:2-5 and answer the questions for today.

Prayer Starter: *"Thank You, Lord, for being my giver of life - the zoe life that I have been studying about. I continue to be amazed at all that You have provided for us in Your Word, and it is there for the taking as I dig in and seek to prayerfully apply what You are teaching me."*

---

1. What are the five truths stated in verse 20?

2. In verse 21, Paul writes that he does not ignore the grace of God. What does that mean practically, and what are some ways to avoid setting aside the grace of God?

3. In Galatians 3:2, how do we receive the Spirit?

4. In Galatians 3:3-5, what additional things do you learn about the flesh versus the Spirit?

Personal Journaling Page
Use this page for your own intentional gratitude,
prayer requests for your group and additional notes.

Lesson Three

Grace Grows the Church

Blessed Assurance

Blessed assurance, Jesus is mine;
Oh, what a foretaste of glory divine!
Heir of salvation, purchase of God,
Born of His Spirit, washed in His blood.

This is my story, this is my song,
Praising my Savior all the day long.
This is my story, this is my song,
Praising my Savior all the day long.

Perfect submission, perfect delight,
Visions of rapture now burst on my sight;
Angels descending, bring from above
Echoes of mercy, whispers of love.

Perfect submission, all is at rest,
I in my Savior am happy and blest;
Watching and waiting, looking above,
Filled with His goodness, lost in His love.

https://www.hymnal.net/en/hymn/h/308

Today we will revisit the story of the woman at the well and her life-changing conversation with Jesus.

Now that you have spent two weeks studying this story along with gaining a deeper understanding of the living water, the abiding life on the vine, the fruits of the Spirit and true transformation of a life yielded to Christ, go back and read the entire story again in John 4:4-42.

In a sense, you have **curated** the information you have studied: you have organized and presented the content, knowledge, and the context of our study.

Prayer Starter: *"Lord, I am so grateful for this story of the woman at the well and how one conversation with Jesus changed everything in her world. As I read it today and wrap up some continuing study, open my eyes to see wonderful things in Your Word. Change me, speak to me, challenge me, and stretch me as I continue to learn from You."*

---

1. Based on your two weeks of deeper study, what new things do you glean from this story?

2. How do you relate to the woman in this story?

3. Summarize how her life was changed by Jesus through one encounter.

4. What surprises you about this encounter?

Lesson 3, Day 2

Jesus continues His conversation with the Samaritan woman; they discuss true worship. We then witness what happens when an entire city hears a powerful testimony from a least-likely source.

Read John 4:19-26 to answer the questions below.

Prayer Starter: *"Lord, teach me what it means to worship You in Spirit and in truth. Open my eyes to see and to learn new things from this conversation with Jesus. May I become more of a genuine worshipper."*

1. Who did the woman perceive that Jesus was, and what did she know about worship?

2. In verses 21-22, what did Jesus teach her about worship?

3. In verses 23-24, list the things you have learned about worship. Use the Greek definitions provided to help you dig deeper.

   Truth: *aletheia. Strong's #225: reality, sincerity, accuracy, integrity, truthfulness, dependability, propriety.*

   Worship: proskuneo.*Strong's #4352: pros means 'toward' and kuneo means 'to kiss', to prostrate oneself, bow down, show reverence, worship, adore.*

4. What amazing thing does Jesus do in verse 26?

This day's study is a glimpse of the white harvest fields.

Read John 4:27-42 to answer the questions today.

Prayer Starter: *"Lord, may I be willing to leave behind the things in my life that hinder my relationship with You, just like the woman at the well. Thank You for 'curating' this story for us so that we can learn from You through the ageless relevancy of Your Word."*

---

1. What two things does the woman do upon Jesus' revelation to her? What is the significance of each one?

2. What are the disciples concerned about and why?

3. What five metaphors does Jesus use to teach His disciples about leading others into truth in verses 34-38? (one per verse)

Lesson 3, Day 4

Our exciting story continues as the transformed Samaritan woman rushes back to her town and becomes an evangelist!

Read John 4:39-42 to answer the questions today.

Prayer Starter: *"Lord, please give me a heart and a burden for the lost - for those who are a part of my life. May I be like the woman in John 4 who wasted no time in sharing her new-found faith with everyone she interacted with. Move me to share You."*

---

1. What were the results of the woman's testimony? How does this challenge you personally?

2. Relate all the events from verses 39-42.

3. What is your number one takeaway from the woman's encounter with Jesus? How will you apply to your own life?

Take the time today to go back over, not only this week's study, but the previous two weeks, *curating* everything you have gleaned from the woman's story.

- What has been your biggest take-away?

- How has her life and response challenged you?

- Has there been a specific way you are praying about applying what you have learned?

- Have you learned anything new about the 'living water' or the zoe life?

- Re-visit the story and read the Scripture passage again.

- Highlight any parts of the past three weeks and come prepared to share with your group.

Personal Journaling Page
Use this page for your own intentional gratitude,
prayer requests for your group and additional notes.

Lesson Four

Curating our Identity in Christ

You Say

I keep fighting voices in my mind that say I'm not enough
Every single lie that tells me I will never measure up
Am I more than just the sum of every high and every low?
Remind me once again just who I am because I need to know

You say I am loved when I can't feel a thing
You say I am strong when I think I am weak
And You say I am held when I am falling short
And when I don't belong, oh You say I am Yours
And I believe, (I) oh I believe (I)
What You say of me (I)
I believe

The only thing that matters now is everything You think of me
In You I find my worth, in You I find my identity, ooh

You say I am loved when I can't feel a thing
You say I am strong when I think I am weak
And You say I am held when I am falling short
When I don't belong, oh You say I am Yours
And I believe, (I) oh I believe (I)
What You say of me (I)
Oh, I believe

Taking all I have and now I'm laying it at your feet
You have every failure God, and You'll have every victory, ooh

You say I am loved when I can't feel a thing
You say I am strong when I think I am weak
You say I am held when I am falling short
When I don't belong, oh You say I am Yours
And I believe, (I) oh I believe (I)
What You say of me (I)
I believe

Oh I believe, ah
Yes I believe, ah
What You say of me
Oh I believe

Have you ever heard of Hetty Green?

She died in 1916 and has gone down in history as "America's Greatest Miser". She left an estate valued at over $100 million dollars, yet she ate cold oatmeal because it cost too much to heat it. Her son had to suffer a leg amputation because she delayed so long in looking for a free clinic, so his case became incurable. She was wealthy, yet she chose to live like a pauper.

Maybe you read this story and shake your head and wonder how it can be that someone would go to those extremes, but how many Christians/*believers*, live this same way? What if we really **believed** everything God said about us?

We have been placed in Christ. The first chapter of Ephesians tells us beautifully and powerfully, how blessed we are, what has been done for us, who we are, and where we are ultimately going.....yet, how many of us live like paupers and don't daily tap into the riches of His glory?

Ephesians 1:3 says: ***"Blessed be the God and Father of our Lord Jesus Christ, who has blessed us with every spiritual blessing in the heavenly places in Christ."***

The Holy Spirit is mentioned many times in this letter because He is the One who channels our riches to us from the Father, through the Son.

Not to know and depend on the Holy Spirit's provision is to live a life of spiritual poverty.

With this in mind, this week we will focus on what the book of Ephesians has to say about who we are in Christ and why we need not live as spiritual paupers.

The Samaritan woman did not stop to think about her past. She had met the Living Lord face-to-face and He 'told her everything she'd ever done'. Jesus transformed her life, and all she wanted to do in response was go and tell everyone else.

We have the blessing of a *'curated'* Bible. Anytime we need to be reminded of our spiritual inheritance, all we need to do is turn to the Word and read the promises and the truth for ourselves. The woman at the well did not have that advantage. What an awesome privilege is ours to spend these weeks in Bible study, to investigate for ourselves, to *curate* what we glean, and to move forward with the life-changing truth of His Word.

Read Ephesians 1:3-14 and answer the questions for today.

Prayer Starter: *"Lord, I praise You for the finished work of Jesus on the cross. Thank You for all He accomplished on my behalf. I want to be a good steward of my spiritual inheritance. I want to live as a believer. Speak to me through Your Word today and continue to seal these truths on my heart."*

---

1. What does Paul praise God for in verse 3, and how do the people of God receive these?

2. List out the spiritual blessings listed in verses 3-6.

3. Jesus told us in John 15:16 that we did not choose Him, but He has chosen us. Verse 4 tells us that we were chosen before the foundation of the world, which reveals that our salvation is wholly of <u>His grace</u>, and not due to anything we ourselves have done. In Ephesians 2:8, Paul declares this same truth. Write it out here and tell why grace is divine favor, joy, and a free gift.

4. In verse 5, the word predestined is used. Look up what that means and explain why it is a blessing.

We are continuing to 'curate' the information provided for us in the Word of God so that we are equipped to flourish.

Read Ephesians 1:3-14 again and answer the questions for today.

Prayer Starter: *"Lord, I rejoice that I am blessed, chosen, holy, blameless, and predestined as an adopted child of Yours, all because of the finished work of Jesus on the cross. I ask You to continue to indelibly write these truths on the deepest part of my heart so that I can flourish and share You with the world."*

---

1. According to verse 6, what is the specific blessing listed for the believer?

   We cannot make ourselves acceptable to God, but He, by His grace, makes us accepted in the Beloved in Christ—this is our eternal position that will never change.

2. Verse 7 lists another amazing blessing for those who are in Christ. This letter from Paul repeatedly insists that the ground of all grace is what, according to:

   • Ephesians 2:16

   • Ephesians 2:13

   • Ephesians 4:32

   • Ephesians 5:25-27

3. Write out the curated blessings that are ours according to verses 8, 9, and 10. What does this mean for us today?

Lesson 4, Days 3 & 4

You will be continuing your journey through Paul's early verses in Ephesians 1. It is vital that believers know and understand their identity in Christ.

Read Ephesians 1:3-14 today and answer the questions.

Prayer Starter: *"Dear Lord, may this study into Your Word, over the next few days, permanently change me so that I embrace my identity in Christ in a fuller way. May I walk in the ways of Your Son and help others to do the same."*

---

1. In verse 11, what are we told that we obtain?

2. What does inheritance mean?

3. Verse 11 also states the truth of how God works things out according to, what?

4. The counsel of His will signifies God's eternal and unchangeable plan. Refer back to verses 1, 5, 9 and 11 and tell how our confidence is established.

5. As we trust in Christ, according to verse 12, what is a natural fruit that comes?

6. Verse 13 shows a three-step progression of trust. Write out the process of salvation here:

7. According to verse 14, who is the "guarantee of our inheritance"? What does guarantee literally mean?

Lesson 4, Day 5

Today you will be reviewing your last four days of study in the first chapter of Ephesians.

I think if I had to call it something, it could be aptly named our 'identity manifesto' - verses packed with truth per square inch describing who we are in Christ.

Take time today to prayerfully review all the information you have 'curated' over the week. Take a yellow highlighter and mark the truths that really spoke to you as you studied.

Now create a list of identity statements from the information you have curated. You can do this in any format that resonates with you. The important thing is that you work from the curated truths you have studied and recorded so far. Feel free to add truths or principles from your study of the woman at the well.

Here are some things to remember about curating your information:
- Make sure your data is retrievable for future use.
- Provide context for the information you share.
- Be selective.
- Identify your key takeaways.
- Create an outline.
- Present your curated information in such a way that it not only impacts your life but others too.

Personal Journaling Page
Use this page for your own intentional gratitude,
prayer requests for your group and additional notes.

Personal Journaling Page
Use this page for your own intentional gratitude,
prayer requests for your group and additional notes.

Lesson Five

What do People Think of Christ?

Jesus Loves Me

Jesus loves me! This I know,
For the Bible tells me so;
Little ones to Him belong;
They are weak, but He is strong.

Refrain:
Yes, Jesus loves me!
Yes, Jesus loves me!
Yes, Jesus loves me!
The Bible tells me so.

Jesus loves me! This I know,
As He loved so long ago,
Taking children on His knee,
Saying, "Let them come to Me."

Jesus loves me still today,
Walking with me on my way,
Wanting as a friend to give
Light and love to all who live.

Jesus loves me! He who died
Heaven's gate to open wide;
He will wash away my sin,
Let His little child come in.

Jesus loves me! He will stay
Close beside me all the way;
Thou hast bled and died for me,
I will henceforth live for Thee.

https://www.godtube.com/popular-hymns/jesus-loves-me/

So far in our study, we have spent time carefully examining the life of a woman who was looking to fill the voids in her life through her relationship with men. One day as she visited her village well, she interacts with Jesus face-to-face and discovers that He is the One to worship in Spirit and in truth.

Through this conversation, the woman is led to salvation in Jesus and she encounters His amazing grace. As a result of this transformative encounter, she then immediately returns to her village and leads others to discover Jesus too.

From our Samaritan woman study, we investigated the rich treasury of the Word as we studied the *'living water'* or the Holy Spirit. This dove-tailed beautifully into the study of *zoe* life, a healthy vine, and fruits of the Spirit.

We've learned about worshiping the Lord in truth. This *curated* study, when fully embraced and applied, naturally bears the fruit of evangelism, which then yields to grace growing the church.

As we continue in the Word, we read truth after truth of our identity in Christ. This produces renewed minds, refreshed by the living Word, and inspires us to move through this world with purpose and the love of God as we share Him with everyone we meet.

We have spent four intentional weeks, curating the information provided as we dig deeper into the Word of God.

Our desire is to *curate so that we can flourish!*

For the remainder of our study, we will continue our investigation into the Word of God and will examine possible dynamics, circumstances, or worldviews that can affect our ability to flourish.

Reach each Scripture provided and answer the questions for each day.

Prayer Starter: *"Lord, I thank You for the amazing and life-changing truth of Your Word. I praise You for the power of Your Word and transforming changes I have already observed in my life. I want to grow and help others to grow too. Speak to me out of Your Word and point out anything in me that needs to change."*

---

1. The word *flourish* conveys what life in Christ is meant to be - enjoying the Lord and living for Him; it's serving with gladness and knowing Christ as our greatest delight. Is this the testimony of your life? Would you say that you have a flourishing lifestyle? Do you have stresses, fears, or irritations that sabotage your joy? Answer these questions and list some of the things in your life that you desire the Lord to address through this study in His Word.

2. Read 2 Timothy 3:1-5. As you look at the list of things Paul has written that hinder a flourishing lifestyle, what is the repeated word he uses in this passage?

3. Write out the list of things Paul shared in the passage above and put them in your own words. How does misplaced love create such difficulty?

4. In 2 Timothy 2: 16-17, what has spread in the world according to Paul, and what did he compare it to?

5. What is the only conclusive source of wisdom, knowledge and understanding concerning ultimate realities according to 2 Timothy 2:15?

6. What are you personally doing in your own life to ensure that you rightly discern the truth of God's Word? Why is this so critical?

Someone has said that we become what we behold.

There is simply no escaping the fact that we're conformed to what we focus on. What are you focusing on? Is it your personal desire to flourish spiritually? If that is your goal, if you want to know joy and peace and to be a fruitful disciple of Jesus, it is important that you are a woman of the Word.

Prayer Starter: *"Lord, I desire to be a woman of Your word. I ask You to cause me to become even more grounded in the Bible in these days I'm living in. I want to know joy and peace and to be a fruitful disciple."*

Read the paragraph below from the book, *Flourish*, along with the passage from Ephesians 2, and then answer the questions.

> *"What do people think of me? By means of our clothes, our weight, our gym routine, the interior of our home, the behavior of our children...we are so easily driven by a craving for an acceptable answer to that question. But in Christ, we are called to ask a different question: What do people think of Christ?*
>
> *When we are driven by a concern for how people perceive Him, we can live free from the bondage of what people think of us. One of the most amazing aspects of being united to Christ by faith is that he actually becomes our very identity, but not until we grasp this truth can we enjoy the freedom of self-forgetfulness."*

1. Read Ephesians 2: 1-10. List the facts of this passage below.

2. What truths can you curate from the incident of Jesus' resurrection and ascension in verses 4-6?

3. This entire Ephesians passage reveals to us that Jesus won for us freedom and the freedom to ask the question daily, ***what do people think of Christ?*** If we take for granted the work Jesus has done for us, we will be consumed with thoughts of ourselves rather than thoughts of Jesus. With that in mind, summarize the verses 4-10 with three possible application steps a believer can make based on our wonderful freedom in Christ.

Prayer Starter: *"Lord, teach me out of your Word today and the next two days as I take a deep dive into the Scripture that highlights Your wisdom, Your blessings, and Your Gospel transformation. May my confidence be firmly placed in You and Your amazing grace as I continue to live for Your glory."*

Read the following passage of Scripture each day for the next three days and answer the questions.

So then, no more boasting about human leaders! All things are yours, ²² whether Paul or Apollos or Cephas or the world or life or death or the present or the future—all are yours, ²³ and you are of Christ, and Christ is of God.

4 This, then, is how you ought to regard us: as servants of Christ and as those entrusted with the mysteries God has revealed. ² Now it is required that those who have been given a trust must prove faithful. ³ I care very little if I am judged by you or by any human court; indeed, I do not even judge myself. ⁴ My conscience is clear, but that does not make me innocent. It is the Lord who judges me. ⁵ Therefore, judge nothing before the appointed time; wait until the Lord comes. He will bring to light what is hidden in darkness and will expose the motives of the heart. At that time each will receive their praise from God.

⁶ Now, brothers and sisters, I have applied these things to myself and Apollos for your benefit, so that you may learn from us the meaning of the saying, "Do not go beyond what is written." Then you will not be puffed up in being a follower of one of us over against the other. ⁷ For who makes you different from anyone else? What do you have that you did not receive? And if you did receive it, why do you boast as though you did not? (1 Corinthians 3:21-4:7 NIV)

1. Why were the people in Corinth boasting about their relationships with certain leaders? Do you think this boasting caused unity in the church? Why or why not?

2. What does Paul reveal in this passage is the root cause for division? (see verse 21 and 4:7)

3. What does Paul urge the Corinthian believers in 4:6 of this passage?

4. What do you learn about pride from this quote from C.S. Lewis, out of his book, *Mere Christianity* and how does it relate to our passage of study?

> *"Pride gets no pleasure out of having something, only out of having more of it than the next person. We say that people are proud of being rich, or clever, or good-looking, but they are not. They are proud of being richer, or cleverer, or better-looking than others. If everyone else became equally rich, or clever, or good-looking there would be nothing to be proud about."*

5. Summarize what you have learned so far today.

Read the passage printed from Day 3 and continue answering the questions:

1. In verses 1 and 2 of 1 Corinthians 4, what does Paul remind the people?

2. In verses 3 and 4 of 1 Corinthians 4, what does Paul want the people of Corinth to know about the Gospel?

3. How do verses 3 and 4 reveal that Paul does not get his sense of identity from other people?

4. Look up 1 Timothy 1:15 and write out what Paul says about himself here:

5. Is Paul speaking in the past-tense or present-tense?

6. Do you think Paul allowed his sins to destroy his sense of identity? Why or why not? (Use Scripture to back up your answer.)

Read the passage from Day 3 and answer the questions:

1. Paul uses the metaphor of a courtroom in this passage. Paul says that the trial is over for him; he is out of the courtroom and the ultimate verdict is in. How could he know and be so confident of that? Use verse 4 to answer.

2. Do you ever feel that your personal performance impacts your walk with the Lord or your standing in the eyes of others? Why or why not?

3. Paul is seeking to explain to the folks in the church in Corinth, that in 'Christianity, the **verdict leads to performance**. It is not the performance that leads to the verdict. In Christianity, the moment we believe, God says over our lives, *"This is my beloved son (daughter) in whom I am well pleased."* (Matthew 3:17)'

    How can Paul teach this with such confidence? Use Romans 8:1 for your answer.

4. The moment we believe, God imputes Christ's perfect righteousness (performance) to us as if it were our own, and He adopts us into His family. In other words, no matter the things we have done - He loves us, accepts us - we do not have to do anything to make us look good. Look up and write out the truths from the following verses that prove Paul's point:

- John 3:16

- Romans 5:1

- John 10:10

- 1 Timothy 2:5

- 1 Peter 3:18

- Romans 5:8

- John 1:12

The verdict is in! We are justified! We are blameless! All glory and honor to God.

This is our ultimate conclusion from the study of this week in the word as we seek to tackle self-centeredness and replace it with *'what do people think of Christ vs. what do people think of me?'* We rejoice in our position in Christ; take the time to read these paragraphs from author and pastor, Tim Keller:

> *"If we were to meet a truly humble person, we would never come away from meeting them thinking they were humble. They would not be always telling us they were a nobody (because a person who keeps saying they are a nobody is actually a self-obsessed person). The thing we would remember from meeting a truly gospel-humble person is how much they seemed to be totally interested in us. Because the essence of gospel-humility is not thinking more of myself or thinking less of myself, it is thinking of myself less.*
>
> *Gospel-humility is not needing to think about myself. Not needing to connect things with myself. It is an end to thoughts such as, "I'm in this room with these people, does that make me look good? Do I want to be here?"*

True gospel-humility means I stop connecting every experience, every conversation, with myself. In fact, I stop thinking about myself. The freedom of self-forgetfulness. The blessed rest that only self-forgetfulness brings.

A truly gospel-humble person is not a self-hating person or a self-loving person, but a gospel-humble person. The truly gospel-humble person is a self-forgetful person whose ego is just like his or her toes. It just works. It does not draw attention to itself. The toes just work; the ego just works. Neither draws attention to itself.

The self-forgetful person would never be hurt particularly badly by criticism. It would not devastate them...it would not bother them. Why? Because a person who is devastated by criticism is putting too much value on what other people think, on other people's opinions. People are either devastated by criticism or they are not devastated by criticism because they do not listen to it. They know who they are and what they think.... they are the self-forgetful, gospel-humble person.... simply thinking of myself less."

"You save the humble, but your eyes are on the haughty to bring them low." (2 Samuel 22:28)

Use the following comparison between a self-centered approach to a God-centered approach. This check list may help you assess how you are responding to various things in your life. Check the ones which most often apply to you.

Self-Centered

___I want it my way

___Is rigid and opinionated

___Gets huffy and defensive if criticized

___Hungers to be admired & praised

___Desires to be the center of attention

___Makes sure others notice good works

___Demands credit

___Indulges self; makes personal comfort a priority

___Practices entitlement thinking: I deserve this; I'm worth it

___Easily offended

___Nurtures resentment

___Inflexible

___Finds it hard to spring back from disappointments

___Tends to excuse her own sin

___Condemns the sin of others

___Obsesses about her obvious failures

___Loves people who love her

God-Centered

___"Your will be done"

___Is flexible and open to others' ideas

___Doesn't take criticism personally; listens & responds if appropriate

___May enjoy praise but doesn't need it; lets others have the limelight

___Performs good deeds without advertising them

___Is willing to sacrifice personal comfort

___Practices gratitude thinking

___Forgives quickly & completely; gives ongoing hurts to God

___Resilient; able to rise above disappointments and use them creatively

___Acknowledges sinful tendencies in self & others, extends God's grace to both

___Accepts God's forgiveness and moves on

___Feels God's heart toward all humanity, is able to love the unlovable

(Joanna Weaver, *At the Feet of Jesus,* pg. 347)

Personal Journaling Page
Use this page for your own intentional gratitude,
prayer requests for your group and additional notes.

Personal Journaling Page
Use this page for your own intentional gratitude,
prayer requests for your group and additional notes.

Lesson Six

I Can Flourish!

I Love You, Lord

I love you, Lord
And I lift my voice
To worship You
Oh, my soul, rejoice!

Take joy my King
In what You hear
Let it be a sweet, sweet sound
In Your ear

Laurie B. Klein

As we wrap up our study of *Curate and Flourish*, this starting point of week six is a good time to reflect for a few minutes on what we have gleaned so far. Our goal has been to dig deep into God's Word and to *curate* or organize, select, and present the truth we have personally studied. From our curating, we are better equipped to *flourish* in our spiritual journey with Jesus.

Last week, we focused on addressing any self-centeredness with the Word of God, and asking ourselves the question: *what do they think of Jesus vs. what do they think of me?*

This week, we will examine two things that can potentially hinder a flourishing lifestyle - a victim mentality and an orphan mentality.

Prayer Starter: *"Lord, help me through Your Holy Spirit and the power of Your Word, to lay aside every weight and enable me to run with perseverance so that I may flourish."*

Bibi Aesha was forced into marriage with a Taliban fighter at age twelve. She endured six years of abuse before managing to escape, only to be caught and ultimately returned to her abusive husband. He punished her by cutting off her nose and ears and leaving her to die on a mountain. Aesha survived, and even though she has a new life in the United States, and a surgically reconstructed face, the abuse she suffered will impact the rest of her life. Aesha is a victim, if there ever was one.

1. Write out your own definition of the word victim. What has shaped your viewpoints or filter on victimhood?

2. Everyone has a story. The trauma of severe abuse can sometimes define a victim's life, but as we unite with Jesus by faith, he frees us from the past and gives us a whole new identity. Write out what the Bible teaches us about this very thing in 2 Corinthians 5:17.

3. The Bible shows us that life in Christ directs us into the future, not the past, and that Jesus himself has established a pattern for us. Read and write out that pattern in Hebrews 12:1-2.

4. What two things are we called to set aside in verse 1, and what are we called to pursue? How can this call free us from living with a victim mentality?

Damage done to us by others, whatever the source of our hurt, is never healed by ignoring the sin that underlies it. Whenever the presence of sin is undermined, a victimhood mentality is able to thrive.

This week's study is not designed to address the deeper issues that a trained counselor would be able to address, but is meant to be a biblical look at the broader issue of a victim mentality itself. What does the Bible have to say about how we are to move forward as we heal? Even if we've experienced deep hurt in our past, how can we *flourish based on what we have curated from our time in the Word?*

Prayer Starter: *"Lord, I long to be a woman who is marked by wholeness due to the presence of Jesus in my heart and life. I want to be a light to everyone I meet, and I want to reflect the healing power of Jesus. Speak to me out of Your living Word today."*

1. From the moment we were joined in faith to Jesus, a process began in our lives where our earlier sufferings (or even current ones) are being transformed by the Spirit. Read Isaiah 61:1-3 and write out the specifics of what happens when we grow in knowledge of our Savior and what salvation means to us.

2. Our trajectory as believers is forward and not backward. In other words, the Lord intends for us to *flourish.* Look up each passage and write how a forward flourishing trajectory is possible.

   • 1 Corinthians 9:24

   • Hebrews 11:8-10

   • Philippians 3:12-14; 20

   • James 1:12

- 1 John 3:2-3

- Revelation 21:1-4

Have you ever been haunted by fear of rejection and failure? Do you ever question where you belong? Do you wonder if you're doing enough for the Lord or others? Do you feel that you cannot ever measure up?

Everyone may feel this way from time to time, but if you consistently deal with thoughts that leave you insecure or feeling abandoned, lonely, or alienated, you may have developed an orphan mindset.

Perhaps you've allowed labels to define you: unwanted, unworthy, unloved, ineffective, needy, clingy. These thoughts and insecurities can limit your flourishing lifestyle.

We will be spending the next three days *curating what the Bible has to say in order for us to flourish!*

Take the time to look up each scripture reference and answer the questions.

Prayer Starter: *"Lord, what a blessing it has been to spend these past few weeks seriously digging into Your Word and curating Your truth so that I can flourish! I long to leave all negative thinking behind and allow Your Word to dominate my thinking, and thus my living. I long for You to heal in the deepest recesses of my soul any victim or orphan mentality that still lives there. May You receive all the glory and all the praise from my flourishing life!"*

---

1. We have spent ample time in this study exploring our Biblical identity. Look up Galatians 4:4-7 and write out the specifics in this passage that contradict a negative orphan mentality.

2. Our spiritual hearts relate to God and as we open our hearts to our heavenly Father's unconditional love, it brings freedom and life. Read Hebrews 12:1-12 and highlight below the beauty of the spiritual fathering done by the Lord as we look to Jesus, the author and finisher of our faith.

Lesson 6, Day 4

1. Read John 14:15-21. List out the imperatives Jesus gave us in this passage.

2. What was the promise Jesus made to us in John 14:18? How can this truth be used to 'combat' the orphan mentality?

3. How do you think the promise of John 14:17 and the final word of verse 21 are crucial to dealing with an orphan mentality?

1. Look up the Scriptures below and tell how each one can be used to communicate a spirit of adoption which leads to a flourishing lifestyle:

   • Proverbs 12:18

   • James 3:5

   • Philippians 4:6

   • Romans 8:26-27

   • Exodus 33:14

   • Proverbs 16:3

   • Jeremiah 29:11

   • 1 Corinthians 14:33

   • 1 Corinthians 2:9

- James 3:14-16

- Hebrews 10:36

2. As a final project based on your entire study of *curate and flourish,* fill in the opposite trait of the flourishing trait listed:

   - Kingdom of God vs _____.

   - Rooted in sonship (daughter-ship) vs. _____

   - Prioritizes identity vs. _____

   - Lives from God vs. _____

   - Influences the world vs. _____

   - Confident in hearing God's voice vs. _____

   - Enjoys God's pleasure without performance vs._____

   - At rest vs. _____

Personal Journaling Page

Use this page for your own intentional gratitude,
prayer requests for your group and additional notes.

Personal Journaling Page
Use this page for your own intentional gratitude,
prayer requests for your group and additional notes.

Curated Information to Help You Flourish

Praying For Your Husband

Offensively (Taking Aggressive Action)	Defensively (A Shield of Protection – Resisting Attack)
Spiritually: • Cause him to uphold Your standard in word and action: grant him courage and boldness. (Eph 6:19) • Give him passionate love, desire and hunger for Your Word, for prayer and for righteousness. (Matt 5:6) • Provide him with greater personal time with You, time to be still, to grow and to be refreshed, so that his roots go down deep in You. (Col 2:6,7) • Fill him with Your Holy Spirit. (Eph 5:18) • Help him to walk in Christ's steps. (I Peter 2:21) • May he wield the sword of the Spirit, which is the Word of God. (Eph 6:17)	**Spiritually:** • Give him a concentrated, thankful heart. (Ps 119:37) • Bring renewal and refreshment into his life so that he will be spiritually sharp. (Ps 51:12) • Clothe him with humility. (I Peter 5:8) • May he wear the belt of truth (walking in truth), the breastplate of righteousness (guarding his heart with all diligence), the shoes of the gospel (always ready to run with the good news), the helmet of salvation (bringing every thought into captivity), and may he always have his shield of faith raised up (in order to quench all the fiery darts of the wicked one). (Eph 6:14-17)
Physically: • Enable him to daily present the members of his body to You as instruments of righteousness. (Rom 6:13) • Enable him to glorify You with his body. (I Cor 6:19,20) • Enable him to offer his body to You as a holy, living sacrifice. (Rom 12:1-2)	**Physically:** • Turn his eyes away from worthless things and preserve his life according to Your Word. (Ps 119:37) • Protect him from evil and deliver him because he knows Your name and has set his love upon You. (Ps 91:14)
Emotionally: • Cause him to unconditionally love and accept others. (I Cor 13) • Enable him to do everything without complaining and arguing. (Phil 2:14) • Enable him to sing and make music in his heart to You, always giving thanks. (Eph 5:19,20) • Enable him to base his self-esteem and self-worth on a clear perspective of You and how You see him. (Col 3:16)	**Emotionally:** • Cause him to daily cast his anxiety on You, knowing how much You care for him. (I Peter 5:7) • Help him to be a patient man and to control his temper. (Prov 16:3)
Mentally: • Cause him to make a covenant with his eyes, not to look lustfully at a female or anything that would provoke lust. (Job 31:1) • Enable him to daily think on the true, noble, right, pure, lovely, admirable, and praiseworthy things. (Phil 4:8) • Grant him wisdom and guidance as he makes plans and decisions, help him not lean on his own understanding but trust You with all of his heart. (Prov 3:5)	**Mentally:** • Enable him to daily submit all of his plans to You and to know within the depths of his soul, that only You carry out those plans. (Prov 16:1, James 4:13-15) • Rid him of a haughty spirit. (Prov 16:18)
Socially: • Enable him to love all people You place in his life, and to always be reaching out to others. (Eph 4:32) • Help him to love and practice hospitality. (Heb 13:2)	**Socially:** • Help him to deal with his frustrations in a godly way. Fill him with wisdom in dealing with people. (Ephesians 4:26; James 1:5) • Fill him with mercy and good fruit. (James 3:17-18)

Praying For Your Children

Thought	Word	Deed/Action	Heart
From their childhood, they would know the Holy Scriptures which are able to make them wise for salvation through faith which is in Christ Jesus. (II Tim 3:15)	They would be taught the word of God from their youth, embracing it in its entirety and declaring Your wonderous works all the days of their lives. (Ps 71:17)	I pray they would always get caught when they have sinned and that they would learn the statutes as a result. (Ps 119: 67,71)	Instill in them souls that follow hard after You, souls that cling passionately to You and souls that thirst for You. (Ps 63: 1,8)
Prevent them from setting their minds on high things, but may they associate with the humble. May they not be wise in their own eyes. (Rom 12:16, James 3:13-18)	Fill then with the joy that can only be received from Your Holy Spirit. (Rom 14:17)	May integrity and honesty be their virtue and their protection. (Ps 25:21)	I pray that You will make them wise in heart and able to receive the commands that are not burdensome. (Prov 10:8, I John 5:3)
May they accept the rebukes in life and gain understanding, increasing in learning. Grant them the fear of You, Lord, and the knowledge of the Holy One. (Prov 9:9-10)	May they not be despised for their youth, but be an example in word, in conduct, in love, in spirit, in faith, in purity – an give attention to reading, to exhortation and to doctrine. (I Tim 4:12-13)	I pray they would desire the right kinds of friends, be protected from wrong associations and be hedged in by God so that they do not find their way to wrong people or wrong places. (Ps 91:9-11, Prov 1:10-11, Hosea 2:6)	May their hearts overflow with hope by the power of the Holy Spirit and may faith grow in their hearts, that by faith they would gain what has been promised them. (Rom 15:13, Luke 17: 5-6, Heb 11)
May they learn to always think the best of people as love thinks no evil. (I Cor 13:5)	Cause them to restrain their lips and not sin with their mouths. (Prov 10:19)	Create in them pure hearts, O God, and let that purity of heart be shown in their actions. (Ps 51:10)	Grant them sound hearts that do not envy others. (Prov 14:30)
May they be single-hearted in loving and applying God's Word, using its wisdom, rather than the world's standards. (Ps 84:10; 119:10)	Let the words of their mouths and the meditations of their hearts be acceptable in your sight, O Lord. (Ps 19:14)	Grant that my children may be generous and willing to share, laying up treasure for themselves as a firm foundation for the coming age. (I Tim 6:18-19)	May they respect and honor those in authority over them and show proper respect to everyone, obeying Your Word. (Rom 13:1, I Peter 2:17)
Help them to daily present their bodies a living sacrifice, holy and acceptable to God, and not be conformed to this world, but be transformed by the renewing of their minds, that they may prove what is that good, acceptable, and perfect will of God. (Rom 12:1-2)	May they be those who rejoice with those who rejoice, and weep with those who weep. (Rom 12:15)	May they hear and heed the rebukes of life, abiding among the wise, in order that they will get understanding. (Prov 15:31-32)	Let all bitterness, wrath, anger, clamor and evil speaking be put away from them, with all malice. Cause them to be kind to others, tenderhearted, forgiving others, even as God in Christ forgave them. (Eph 4:31-32)
Cause them to be aware of their own vulnerability to temptation so that they would watch and pray. (Matt 26:41)	May their mouths be instruments of righteousness, blessing both God and man. (James 3:1-12)	Protect them from the evil one in every area of their lives. (John 17:15)	May they love Your law and meditate on it all the day. (Ps 119:17)
May they meditate and think upon all that which is true, noble, just, pure and lovely. (Phil 3:8)	May they store up understanding and knowledge, speaking words of wisdom and justice. (Ps 37:30)	Cause them to be kind and not envy others, behave rudely, or seek their own interests. (I Cor 13:4)	May they never leave their first love, but serve the Lord with undivided hearts all the days of their lives. (Rev 2:1-7)

Having a Meaningful Quiet Time

Attitude is everything!
- Come before God with expectancy, anticipation and eagerness to hear from Him.
- Come into His Presence with reverence.
- Get wide awake and alert first! The best preparation for quite time in the morning begins with the night before.
- Cultivate a willingness to obey Him, no matter what His leading is.

Select a Specific Time
- Choose the time when you are at your best.
- Give God the best part of your day.
- Whatever time you set, be consistent in it.
- If you have never had a consistent quiet time with God, start with 7 minutes a day and let it grow naturally. All of us can spend 7 minutes!

Follow a simple plan that works for you.
- **If you aim at nothing, you will hit nothing.** In order to have your time alone with the Lord be meaningful, it's important to have a plan for meeting with Him.
- **Relax**: Wait on God; be still and know that He is God (Ps 46:20); quiet yourself before Him.
- **Request**: Pray briefly and ask Him to cleanse your heart and guide your time together: "Search me, O God", "Open my eyes to see wonderful things in your Word." (Ps 139:23, Ps 119:18)
- **Read**: This is where your conversation with God begins. He speaks to you through His Word.
- **Reflect**: Remember and medicate on the Scriptures you have read. Journal what you have gleaned out of the verse or passage.
- **Request**: After God has spoken to you through His Word, speak to Him in prayer, based on what you have learned, heard and received.

A simple acrostic to aid in your prayer time:
- **P-Praise the Lord**: Begin your prayer time by praising God for Who He is and what He has done.
- **R-Repent of your sins**: This is the prayer of confession, asking Him to enable you to turn away from any revealed sin.
- **A-Ask** for yourself and others: This is the time of petition and intercession.
- **Y-Yield yourself to God's will**: Reaffirm the Lordship of Jesus Christ in your life, and your willingness to submit, obey and trust Him.

Remember: Your main purpose in having a daily quiet time with the Lord is to get to know Him. This is not a ritual but a <u>relationship</u> with the Living Lord!

Works Cited

The New Spirit-Filled Life Bible. Nashville, TN. Thomas Nelson Publishers, 2002. Print.

The Freedom of Self-Forgetfulness. Timothy Keller. 10Publishing, 2012.

Renner, Rick. Sparkling Gems from the Greek. Tulsa: Teach All Nations Publishing, 2003.

Strong, James, (Corrected by John R. Kohlenberger, III and James A. Swanson). The Strongest Strong's Exhaustive Concordance of the Bible. Grand Rapids: Zondervan, 2001.

Flourish: How the love of Christ frees us from self-focus. Lydia Brownback. Crossway, 2019.

Called to Reign: Living and loving from a place of rest. Leif Hetland. Convergence Press, 2017,

At the feet of Jesus. Joanna Weaver. Waterbrook Press, Colorado Springs, Colorado. 2012.

THROUGH THE WORD

Flourish Through the Word is a community of women of all ages who gather weekly to worship, pray, study the Bible together, and build relationships. From these weekly gatherings, women are then equipped to move out into their arenas of influence and be a light for Jesus.

Flourish is a *501C3* ministry that is supported by the material fees charged for the studies and private donations. If you'd like to find out more about the ministry or make a tax-deductible donation, please visit **flourishthroughtheword.com**. Donations can be made online or by mailing a check to:

Flourish Through the Word
2020 Maltby Road, PMB 240
Bothell, WA 98021

On our website are various Bible study teaching sessions based on the studies our community has done together. These are easily viewed for use in home, church, or small group. Please contact our ministry for more details.

Flourish is delighted to provide a podcast that features Marjie and her sister, Leigh, plus guests. Each short podcast highlights topics that pertain to the daily lives of women as they seek to honor Jesus with every aspect of their lives. Find us at **flourishthroughtheword.com** and stay tuned for new epidsodes regularly.

About the Author

Marjie Schaefer believes the Word of God is relevant, powerful, transformational, and life-giving to every single human being on the planet. She has spent her adult life investing in others and inviting them to join her in this pursuit of deeper truth. Marjie has published several studies available on Amazon: *Life Upon Life, Come to the Table, Dare to Believe, Your Story Matters, Choose Joy, I Believe in the Name of Jesus,* and several others.

Marjie and her husband Steve, live in the Seattle area and have four grown children, a daughter-in-law and grandson, Jack.

CPSIA information can be obtained
at www.ICGtesting.com
Printed in the USA
LVHW061259230120
644573LV00015B/411